Fish Tales
I Used to be Mean
by Sue Theisen

I Used to be Mean Copyright © 2011 by Susan L. Theisen. All rights reserved

No part of this book may be reproduced or transmitted in any form or by any means, electronic or mechanical, including photocopying, recording, or by any information storage and retrieval system, without written permission from the publisher.

PRINTED IN THE UNITED STATES OF AMERICA
Cumming, GA

Being someone that was a victim of bullying as a child,
I know first hand the impact that it can cause.

Bullying is NOT okay. Picking on others because they are different or aren't in your circle of friends is not okay. Calling people names is not okay. Physically or emotionally abusing people is not okay. If you are doing these things stop. If this is happening to you tell someone. Keep saying it until someone listens and helps.

Children go to school to learn. School is supposed to be a safe place for students. I hope this book can somehow help to make that a reality for all kids.

With today's technology, bullying is now reaching new heights, and is having a distressing effect on our children.
It needs to stop, NOW.

I would like to dedicate this book, to all the children, that have suffered at the hands of another. Please know that you are not alone.

I would like to thank my husband Jim for his support and kindness.

Thank you Kari for helping me put some of the finishing touches on this book.

Thanks again Daniel. You Rock!

When I was a younger fish,
swimming in school.
I picked on other fish.
I thought it was cool.

I'd chase them through kelp beds,
and call them all bad names.

I never allowed them
to join in our games.

I'd scare them with fish hooks,
harpoons and big nets.

I never felt badly,
or had any regrets.

I'd pull on their gills
and take their lunch money.
When they couldn't eat,
I thought it was funny.

I'm not really sure why I did it, you see.
Except, perhaps,
they seemed different than me.

How they were different,
I didn't really know.
But, they didn't seem to fit in,
or go with the flow.

I didn't really think
what I was doing was wrong,
Because, most of the time, others
just went along.

Some tried to help those
who'd been picked on by me.
But, most would just swim away,
as if they didn't see.

I never thought about
the damage I'd done.
Then, one day I saw it,
on the face of my son.

When he came home from school,
his head hanging down,
His beautiful smile had been replaced
by a frown.

I could see all the pain in
my little boy's eyes.
It was the very same pain
I saw in those past fishes lives.

I asked him what it was,
that was making him sad.
He told me that other fishes
were treating him bad.

I could tell he needed to know,
about my past and my scene.
So, I took a deep breath and said,
"Son, I used to be mean."

"Why, Daddy, why?
Why were you so cruel?
Why did you hurt all those
fishes in school?"

I said, "I didn't know,
but I'm not like that now.
If I could take it all back,
I'd do it somehow."

It's clear to me now,
how awful I'd been.
And, how I hate the fact
that it was happening to him.

I made sure to tell him,
he'd done nothing wrong.
And, that I can remember
how hard it is getting along.

We worked with his counselor,
and after awhile,
His confidence grew,
and so did his smile.

He now holds his head high
and is seldom blue.
Sometimes, he even
helps the other fishes, too.

I guess when you're young,
you really don't see,
That everyone just wants
to be happy and free.

In school, the little ones are
there to learn and have fun.
Not to have other fish be
a threat, tease or shun.

If kids are being mean to you,
or treating you bad,
Be sure that you tell your
mom or your dad.

Tell all your teachers,
and school counselor, too.
Because, we all deserve respect,
and that includes you.

Now, if you are a bully,
it's just not okay.
It's likely that you, too,
will regret it someday.

Treat others the way that
you want to be treated,
And, you will find before
school is completed,
That, by being kind,
you'll never go wrong,
Because all little fish want
is to feel safe and belong.

The End